CAUTION

FUNNY SIGNS AHEAD

RoadTrip America®

D1015942

CAUTION
FUNNY SIGNS
AHEAD

RoadTrip America®

**Megan Edwards
& Mark Sedenquist**

Ulysess Press

Published in the U.S. by
Ulysses Press
P.O. Box 3440
Berkeley, CA 94703
www.ulyssespress.com

ISBN-10: 1-56975-687-2
ISBN-13: 978-1-56975-687-4
Library of Congress Control Number 2008904132

Design and layout: what!design @ whatweb.com

Editorial: Claire Chun, Nick Denton-Brown, Erica Hellerstein, Bryce Willett

Printed in China by China One Printing

10 9 8 7 6 5 4 3 2 1

Distributed by Publishers Group West

INTRODUCTION

You know you're addicted to hilarious road signs when you bring a 7-ton, 32-foot monster of a motor home screeching to a halt on the New Jersey Turnpike in the middle of rush hour just to snap a shot of a misspelled hazard warning. What can we say? We're junkies. We've done this and a whole lot worse. That's the power our favorite prey holds over us.

While we don't usually take road trips just to capture funny signs, we never take a road trip without keeping an eye out for them. Some people like to collect teaspoons or T-shirts, but for us, the best mementos of two-lane odysseys are photos of strategically burnt-out neon, cunningly rearranged letters, baffling grammar, ironic juxtapositions, and spelling from another planet. Sure, we take plenty of pictures of sunsets and scenery, but friends are a lot more eager to look at our slide shows when the postcard panoramas are sandwiched between pictures of funny signs.

Ever since we hit the road back in 1994 and bagged our first highway howler, we've been on the hunt for more. If anything, our addiction to capturing a mixed-up marquee or a billboard blunder has gotten worse over the years. We've driven hundreds of miles out of our way, climbed through barbed wire, driven into a flash flood, ignored "keep out" signs, and yes, even stopped on the New Jersey Turnpike during rush hour. Once you've been bitten by the funny sign bug, there is no cure.

The great news is we're not alone! After we put our fledgling collection of funny signs on the web back in 1996, other lovers of roadside esoterica began sharing the results of their own adventures in sign stalking. This book reflects over a decade's worth of collecting, and it includes images from no fewer than 92 photographers. Their pictures hail from all over the United States, Canada, and beyond. Like us, these sign hunters have often gone to remarkable lengths to capture their quarry. We salute not only their photographic skill but also their vision, driving ability, perseverance, and willingness to take abuse from the other occupants in their vehicles (apparently not everyone thinks it's a good idea to stop on the Jersey Turnpike). Timing is critical, too—sign makers sometimes realize and correct their errors. So here's a special toast to those who captured a brilliant specimen before it was doomed to extinction by a second thought.

One of the most delightful features of a road trip is the element of surprise, the feeling you get when you turn a corner and see something that makes you shout out "OMG! Stop! Where's the camera?"

We hope you get that feeling as you turn the pages of this book. And if it makes you go out in search of funny signs, remember two things:

1) Stopping in middle of a busy freeway could result in a hefty fine.

2) But if you're going to do it anyway...send us the pictures!

Megan Edwards & Mark Sedenquist
RoadTripAmerica.com

September 2008

SIGNS

Look, Honey! It's a herd of oily-chested Australians!
Megan Edwards in Las Vegas NV

Next stop: Eternal Damnation.
Gerald Thurman in Hope AZ

You can never be too careful with those do-it-yourself colonoscopy kits.
Joe Loehr in Little Bighorn MT

We're not even going to tell you the farmer joke that goes with this sign....
Mark Holloway near Hoover Dam AZ

Don't worry, it's all part of an elaborate plan to confuse the terrorists.
Michael Reardon in Cleveland OH

We have crabs, too, but we don't like to brag.
Jim McIntyre in Adamstown PA

The sounds of the wild.
Wendy Alexander in Acadia National Park ME

Sounds awesome...if you're Davy Crocket.
Megan Edwards in Gillett AR

Wash before handling.
Rod & Judy Ness in Wilmington NC

Head Florist: Lorena Bobbitt
Bethany Heginbotham in Fishers IN

But how far to Mars?
Megan Edwards near Mars PA

The Few, The Proud, The Chalupas.
Janelle M. Chang in Helena MT

In a town as pretty as Fort Laramie how could anybody be a sorehead?
Geneviève Lauzière in Ft. Laramie WY

World's Least Useful Bathroom.
Heather Aday in San Antonio FL

Give me an H! Give me an A! Give me an M! Goooo HAM!
Megan Edwards in Las Vegas NV

If they were faster, it would be better sport.
Megan Edwards in Westerville OH

Cat Crap or Zinrdif? Hmmm, I think I'll take my chances with the "Zinrdif."
Erik Hollander in Wichita KS

From the people who brought you Books on Tape For The Deaf.
Ken Bell in Concord MA

Wave goodbye...
Pamela Alcorn in Cannon Beach OR

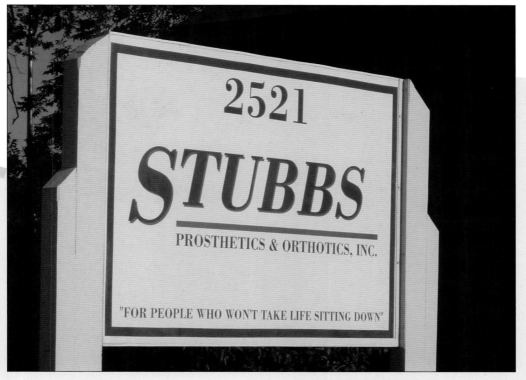

2521

STUBBS

PROSTHETICS & ORTHOTICS, INC.

"FOR PEOPLE WHO WON'T TAKE LIFE SITTING DOWN"

A name that somehow comes up short.
Robert B. Blalock in Chattanooga TN

Hazards on the highway of life.
Pat Mount in Yellowstone National Park WY

Take two aspirin and stretch out in the parking lot.
Eric James Miller in Las Vegas NV

It says "Que gringo estupido."
David and Natalie Rayburn in Tampa FL

Seems like you can't take a corner in Oatman anymore without running into a Cattle Abduction.
Megan Edwards near Oatman AZ

Wheeeeeeeeeeee!
Suzanne Deans in Jackson MS

It's also One-Way and No U-turns.
Tom Newton in Wamic OR

The customer is always burned.
Liisa Sakari in Houghton MI

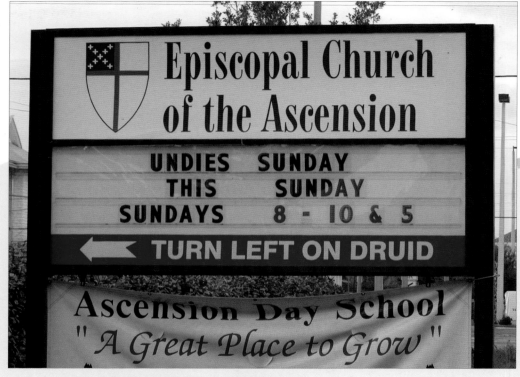

Episcopalians fight declining membership.
Peter Yauch in Clearwater FL

Great, now the humped lions are
going to know exactly where to
look for them.
Tami D. Cowden in Leicestershire UK

Grab a Snickers, because you're
gonna be here for awhile.
Megan Edwards in Redwoods National Park CA

Sooner or later, everyone passes through here.
Kevin Jemmott in Albany GA

But what if we're the last people on Earth?
Megan Edwards in Tehachapi CA

What about the actresses?
Myke Elliott in Moncton NB

SINCE 1706

Blue Ball Hotel

Over 300 years of agony.
Megan Edwards in Blue Ball PA

Um...Yes, you are.
Ruth Mormon in Amherst NY

Thanks, I'll use the can.
Mark Holmes near Lake Hodges CA

Of course he did. If he can walk across water he can probably make blackjack.
Megan Edwards in Jean NV

Couldn't they just blindfold them?
Daniel Janes near Kilmersdon UK

Just don't pee on the electric eels.
Matthew Rounis in Phoenix AZ

Okay, but what's his name?
Daryl Gruber in Highland MI

At the last minute, Subway decided to go with the "Jared" commercials instead.

Michael H. Dickman in Bremen Germany

Six kilometers? But I want my head smashed in nowwww!
Megan Edwards near Fort Macleod AB

Where the Burghers get together.
Jim McIntyre near Leuven Belgium

Hurry! Blondes going fast!
Geneviève Lauzière in Lyndonville VT

Rooms by the hour.
R. Charles Siple in Rifle CO

But do they get a complimentary imaginary continental breakfast?
Geneviève Lauzière in Chamberlain SD

Available by the pair.
Rod Ness in Maple WI

Where Superman parks.
Megan Edwards in Southfield MI

Come on in for a beaver shot!
Phillip Stringer in Cassville MO

Instead of flowers, you just pee on their grave.
Megan Edwards near Calico CA

Uncle Sam wants to make you a hero.
Robert E. Oshel in Cleveland OH

Couldn't they have squeezed "Ave." in there, too, just to be safe?
Tom Brookover in Wolverine MI

GASTROENTEROLOGY
&
ENDOSCOPY

P.R. BIKKASANI, M.D.
ANIL K. RAM, M.D.
PAUL A. HELLSTERN, M.D.

This guy was born to be a proctologist.
Kevin J. in Crystal River FL

Manly men need not apply.
Michael Jessie in Westfield NJ

But what about peenig?
Michael Bono in Elgin IL

Boiling Springs School

COGRATULATIONS
TO BEE WINNERS
ALLANNA VOSS
AND
ANDI MORGAN

The losers got to put up the sign.
Tracye Morgan in Boiling Springs NC

You get what you pay for.
Michael Bono in Streamwood IL

Specializing in mullets.
Erik Hollander in Chicago IL

What is this, Amsterdam?
Peter Yauch in Clearwater FL

Where are the cocaine and hookers?
Megan Edwards in Las Vegas NV

Do you get paid overtime for pulling a double shit?
Matt S. in Rochester NH

Fun neighborhood.
Megan Edwards in Sandy Valley NV

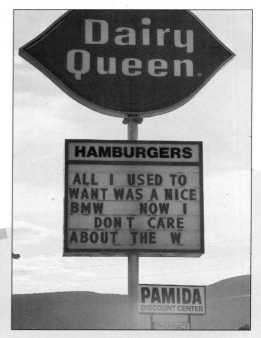

Thanks so much for sharing.
Nancy G. Murphy in Livingston MT

Bring your bongos!
Megan Edwards in Cool CA

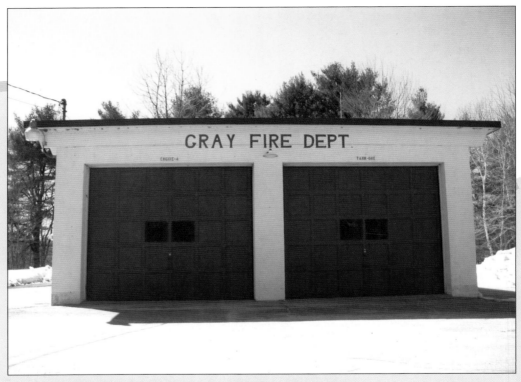

Exposure to intense heat may cause colorblindness.
Geneviève Lauzière in Gray ME

FREE
SMELLS
EXTREMELY
FAST
DELIVERY

Cheese cut while you wait!
Megan Edwards in Las Vegas NV

Don't drink downstream.
Jack Eiermann in Hilo HI

It wasn't bad until the refrigerators went on the blink.
Julie Suneson in Hot Springs AR

You should try the chef's special!
Megan Edwards in Rosemead CA

Flash your breasts if you love Mother Nature!
Nancy Koch Winter in Manhattan KS

EXIT 35

1249

Baptist
Pumpkin Center

Praise the gourd.
Jim Pankey in Pumpkin Center LA

Hardman Gynecology Center

Medical & Surgical Disorders of Women

William M. Hardman, M.D.

He's a real stand-up guy.
Rich & Steven Madow in Lake Wales FL

And you thought they were a myth.
Geneviève Lauzière in Normal IL

Not very subtle, but at least the bad guys know where to meet.
Megan Edwards in North Las Vegas NV

Sometimes it's been hard.
Laura Weddle in Boise ID

Get a piece of the Rock of Ages.
Janet & Robert Daniel in San Diego CA

The Highway to Hell.
Megan Edwards in Shiprock NM

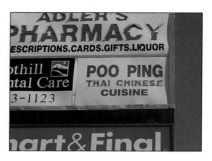

MSG is the last thing you need to worry about here.
Megan Edwards in La Crescenta CA

You'd think that it would be more impressive.
Megan Edwards in Las Vegas NV

And if it doesn't fit perfectly, return it for a full refund.
Ruth Mormon in Buffalo NY

You might want to stay on the sidewalk.
Megan Edwards near Lost Hills CA

← CARNIVAL TODAY BEHIND DUMP

As if carnivals weren't already trashy enough.
Dan Bentley in Oaks PA

Life summed up in four words.
Allan Llewellyn in Anthem AZ

Don't bother kissing him. He's a dead end.
Julia Alexander in Yosemite National Park CA

No, no, that's not Satan. That's just Johnny Knoxville with wings.
Megan Edwards in Lathrop Wells NV

Just don't ask him to stand behind his work.
Peter M. Lighthall in Chocowinity NC

You mean that fast-moving, wet, blue thing isn't part of the road?
Stephanie Casey in Johnston IA

Neighborhood Watch participation has been through the roof.
Megan Edwards in North Las Vegas NV

Real estate bargains downwind...
Megan Edwards near Olanche CA

Man, I knew we should have turned left at Shortcut Road.
Peter Yauch in Seminole FL

Cheerios are on aisle seven, right next to the strychnine and rat poison.
Megan Edwards in Centerville OH

OK! Shoot me one!
Christopher Hayter in Sunrise FL

Thanks, but I think I'll pass.
Melissa Wical in Bellefontaine OH

What marketing genius decided to make the company's color orange?
Megan Edwards in Las Vegas NV

You'll be itching for seconds!
Karen Ditello in Columbus OH

The Department of the Obvious must be working overtime this week.
Megan Edwards in Victorville CA

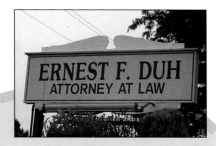

I hope he's the public defender because nobody would ever choose to hire this guy.
Megan Edwards in Phillipsburg NJ

The Buford sisters work for cheap.
Megan Edwards in Sharonville OH

Plug your nose and dive right in!
Steve Loopstra in Brooklyn Center MN

Old oil companies never die—they just slowly burn out.
Megan Edwards in Las Vegas NV

Aaaaaaaaah!
Peter Harvey near Hilt CA

88.8% guaranteed!
Megan Edwards in Signal Hill CA

The customer is always bruised.
Alexander Rose in Carson City NV

Ask about their spelling policy.
Megan Edwards in Las Vegas NV

High gas prices aren't the only tragedy in America.
Erik Hollander in Wichita KS

This is why you should always check Urban Dictionary before naming a restaurant.
Paul Wood in Moore OK

Good thing they're not Catholic, or the confessions would never end.
Megan Edwards in Beaverlick KY

A. Funny Name.
Megan Edwards in Mars PA

Michael Jackson was the chief investor.
Erik Hollander in Jacksonville FL

Nice to see they're giving these ladies a day job.
Barbara Morgan in Ellison Bay WI

You'd think so, too, if you were making hazard pay.
Megan Edwards in Nice CA

For those suffering from hoof-in-mouth disease.
Michael Bono in Elgin IL

Well, that narrows it down.
Megan Edwards in Panguitch UT

How Mary's dad keeps the boys away.
Jeff Winter in Bethany KY

No fiancé? No problem!
Rebecca Burns in Middletown RI

**Well, maybe if you're cute
and blonde.**
Phillip Stringer in Diamond MO

**Every woman's
favorite superhero.**
Katchaya in Fall River MA

Back inna old country, everybody eata bleu balls.
Peter Yauch in Seminole FL

The only way this sign could be funnier is if it was next to a Jiffy Lube.
Tara Chando in East Haven CT

A place that keeps tongues wagging.
Megan Edwards near Big Bone KY

The straight poop on highway conditions.
Ken Rhinehart in Pomona CA

Sleep here, get stuffed.
Sari Boudreau in McAdam NB

It's how granny keeps her costs down.
Michael Metzing in Louisville KY

For the upwardly mobile.
Megan Edwards in Harrisburg PA

Who wants a tour?
Mark Holloway in El Paso TX

They decided to go with accuracy over spelling.
Richard Cies in Oklahoma City OK

It really is a different planet over there.
Megan Edwards near Earth TX

My dog is a genius! I didn't even have to tell him to stay off the grass!
Pat Mount near Lordsburg NM

Just don't try to phone home.
Steve Berger in Flagstaff AZ

Welcome to America!
Megan Edwards near Calico CA

And he reads Playboy for the articles.
Benjamin Klein in Key Biscayne FL

Don't even ask.
Peter Yauch in Atlanta GA

A meal that stays with you.
Anna Vernicek in Atlas IL

Half-off specials with proof of paternity.
Robert Ferguson in Branson MO

They'll cost you thousands of dollars, never clean up after themselves, and stick you in a nursing home when you're old.
Megan Edwards in Boothbay Harbor ME

At least they won't nickel-and-dime you.
Valerie Estes in Sun Valley NV

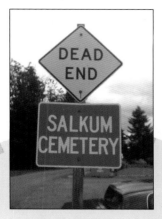

Oh is that what a cemetery is?
Bill R. in Salkum WA

The children would be faster, but it's hard to run when your legs have been gnawed to bloody stumps.
Erik Hollander in Jacksonville FL

At the University of Philip Morris.
Don Moore in San Antonio TX

Toyota's not messing around.
Clint Anglin in Troy NY

Take a deep guzzle and count to 10 RPMs.
Pat Mount in Belmont CA

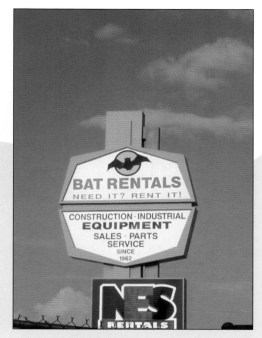

Need a bat but don't want to buy? Come on down to Bat Rentals, where we can set you up with the perfect leasing option to meet all your bat needs.
Megan Edwards in Las Vegas NV

Everything you need for your trip.
Shea Listwon in Meridian MS

Hot new franchise opportunity!
Ed Higginbotham in Houston TX

Desperately seeking the man in the moon.
Megan Edwards in Rainier OR

Best finger in town!
Megan Edwards in Las Vegas NV

It must be a school zone.
Megan Edwards near Baker CA

You know, just in case you were driving upside down.
Mark Sedenquist in Barstow CA

Vive la derrière!
Steve Skopyk in Frenchman Butte SK

So what the hell is it?
Peter Yauch in Union WV

The Great White Swale.
Ron Gillentine near Baker CA

Lions, tigers, and felons, oh my!
Megan Edwards near Buckeye AZ

Good thing they cleared that up.
Christina Moore near Atigun Pass in AK

I bet the mayor's name is Joe.
Megan Edwards in Cool CA

Whatthehell Way was already taken.
Aleisha Dawn Rosse in Port Medway NS

Vegetable oil is for hippies. This is Texas, dammit!
Megan Edwards in Van Horn TX

Don't be late. They won't start without you.
Cindy Brown in Effingham IL

Accountants welcome!
Jeff Smith in Bland VA

Watch your frickin' step.
Terry & Carole Moran near Toronto ON

Like women need any more of those!
Jillian Imilkowski in Chicago IL

What if it was on fire? Or covered with landmines? Would it be safe then?
Larry Abramson in Byhalia MS

It sounds delicious, but does it float?
Geneviève Lauzière in Bethel ME

Then toot on down the road.
Megan Edwards in Tipton IN

It's a fishy habit.
Megan Edwards in Las Vegas NV

Stuff? I was just looking for some stuff!
Megan Edwards in Little Rock AR

OMG! Have you, like, seen the new Gucci ass? Soooo much better than Louis Vuitton's!
Phil Kappen in Sioux Falls SD

You can't say they didn't warn you.
Megan Edwards in Little River CA

UNDISCOVERED SILVER VEIN

This hidden vein of silver ore in the middle of the road was exposed when the road was bladed in the 1950s. The Vein was missed by the old timers and is an example of how all the outcropped veins looked when they were discovered by Jim Butler in May of 1900. The brown rhyolite can be seen on each side (the "walls" of the vein) with the quartz in the center. The black is the manganese oxide and silver ore.

Shhh...Don't tell anybody.
Megan Edwards in Tonopah NV

Latin Lovers here! Hot off the press! Get your Latin Lover here!
Peter Yauch in Largo FL

...And I'm itching to share.
Rod & Judy Ness in Poplar Branch NC

The price is right, but how pretty is she?
Myke Elliott in Moncton NB

For some reason, Boring never took off the way Portland did.
Joel Lecht in Boring OR

Burger & small fries.
Jim Pankey in Houston TX

This is what happens when you don't pay your taxes.
Doug Bandos in St. Augustine FL

The sign must have been written by a crash survivor.
Paul Wood in Guthrie OK

Just so you know.
Stephen Ault in Brunswick ME

They'll stop at nothing!
Barbara Morgan in Bisbee AZ

Don't you hate it when they do that?
Myke Elliott in Halifax NS

TURN ⟶
FOR 500 WEST
SOUTH OF
1200 SOUTH

Did you catch that?
Megan Edwards in Delta UT

Made with real STDs.
Jillian Imilkowski in Two Rivers WI

Trespassing up until this point is fine, however.
Tom Brookover near Holly MI

You can look, but you better not touch.
Megan Edwards near Anderson Junction UT

Chuck Norris, DDS.
Megan Edwards in Las Vegas NV

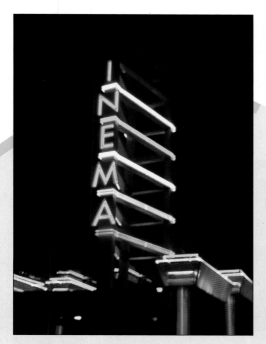

You really have to see it on the big screen to appreciate it.
Megan Edwards in Las Vegas NV

The circle of life.
Megan Edwards in Pomeroy WA

The food isn't great but the portions are tremendous!
Megan Edwards in Mesquite NV

Don't stop until you can see your reflection.
Megan Edwards in Golden Valley AZ

Russian (dressing) Roulette.
Margaret Feit in Port Clinton OH

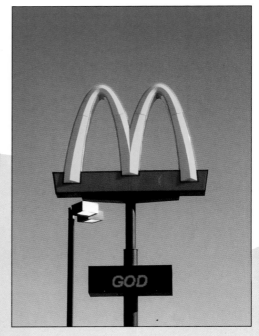

**Give us this day our
daily McBread.**
Megan Edwards in Shiprock NM

Technically it's a smash, but they didn't have two Ss.
Megan Edwards in Las Vegas NV

But, honey, I only go there for the oxygen.
Megan Edwards in Pahrump NV

Others just call them "hamburgers."
Megan Edwards in Boulder City NV

Um...No thank you.
Erik Hollander in Eddyville KY

Real men only hunt children with handguns.
Douglas Sedgwick in Bath ME

Come get a hummer on Ho Road!
Gerald Thurman in Carefree AZ

Are you sure you want to Super-Size that?
Megan Edwards in Marienville PA

AUTHOR'S BIO

RoadTripAmerica.com was founded in 1996 by Mark Sedenquist and Megan Edwards. Now in its second decade "on the road and online," RTA is an interactive resource for planning road trips in North America and sharing tips, routes, and destinations. RTA also boasts a large and ever-expanding gallery of funny signs. Submissions are welcome and encouraged!

SUBMISSIONS
Got a funny sign to share with the world? Wanna see it in **Caution Funny Signs Ahead II**? Send it to us at RoadTripAmerica.com. But be sure to set your digital camera to the highest resolution so it'll stand out on the page. Send photos as attachments to **mark@roadtripamerica.com** and you might just see your name in print.